how to write a poem

and some other poems

SARAH HOLDING

FIREHORSE

Copyright © 2021 Sarah Holding

Published by Firehorse Enterprises Ltd

Cover design by Firehorse,
Illustrations by the author.

British Library Cataloguing Data
A catalogue record for this book is available from
the British Library.

ISBN 978-1916307063

All rights reserved by the author.

Poems in this collection may only be stored,
reproduced or transmitted with the prior
permission of the author in writing, or
under the terms of the Copyright Licencing Agency.

The poems in this collection are works of fiction and
any resemblance to any person, living or dead, or
actual events, is purely coincidental.

Printed and bound in the UK by TJ Books.

Typeset in 12pt Minion Pro and 16pt Heiti TC.

contents

how to write a poem	6
home life	7
birthday present	8
ordymantydollygolly	9
I ran away from school today	10
animal phobia	11
time	12
treehouse	13
jumpy heart	15
advice for campers	17
outage outrage	18
another time	19
medal	20
(to be read with clenched teeth)	21
Ray's ghost	22
dustbinman	23
things that are brilliant	24
tall story	25
dogs in cars	26
sister selfie	27
home alone	28
new girl	29
a lazy story (with no letter e)	30
when I'm older	31
hummus	32
what's in paradise?	33
weird, actually	34
apostrophe, catastrophe	35
last Christmas	36

seabean	37
magpie	38
on Sundays	39
playing	40
jeepers creepers!	41
when my hair grows long	42
London	43
wrong names	44
indoor voices	45
in the loft	46
babies	47
things I wouldn't do if I were you	48
monopoly	49
a poem about running	50
fireworks	51
snow	52
mazes	53
duffel coat	54
TV animals	55
beans on toast	56
spider's web	57
some pages for your own poems	58
about the author	64

*To my Dad
and the generations of poetry
lovers who went before you,
with love and thanks
for reading poems to me
when I was little.*

how to write a poem

you write the first line
and decide if you like it
then another idea pings inside your head
and you try to write it down quickly
before it runs away

then you leave a little space
(you don't have to
if you don't want to)
and maybe try to use
an interesting word
like mellifluous

(you can cross out the interesting words later
if they don't sound right)

it's sometimes liquorice
to use a word
but not in the way
it's supposed to be

adults never seem to agree
about whether a poem should rhyme
so try to mix it up a bit
and don't rhyme all the time

some poems get a proper ending
and some just
end

home life

Mum says, make your bed
but I don't want to

Dad says, blow your nose
but I say g-no

Joe says, grow up
but I'm not ready yet

Nan says, come here
but… gimme a hug

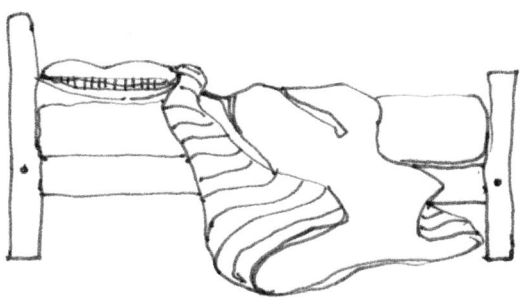

birthday present

maybe I'll get her a pink pony
perhaps she'd prefer a blue one
what about a cheese toastie?
no, too messy to wrap
I could buy her a nice peg
to stop her snoring at night
or a dandelion clock
to blow, instead of candles
she wants a new teatowel
but that's boring
and Aunt Aida isn't
she's lovely but lonely
so I think I'll get her
a miracle

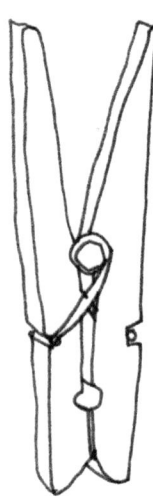

ordymantydollygolly

I stood inside the shop and shouted
ordymantydollygolly!
but no one knew what I meant
my Mum looked in her shopping basket
and the shop assistant said
I don't think we sell that madam

I ran inside the library and yelled
ordymantydollygolly!
but no one knew what I meant
my Mum gazed at the bookshelves
and the librarian said
we don't have that book madam

I jumped onto the bus and bawled
ordymantydollygolly!
but no one knew what I meant
my Mum peered inside her purse
and the bus driver said
this bus doesn't go there madam

I stomped up to my bedroom and barked
ordymantydollygolly!
but no one knew what I meant
my Teddy glared at the other toys
and then at last he whispered
dollygollynipnop?

I ran away from school today

I ran away from school today
deep into the woods
I hid in an old tree trunk
to get my breath back

I ran away from school today
for a moment it felt good
to picture all their faces
scared and worried sick

I ran away from school today
it wasn't hard to do
until I got kind of lost
and then I cried a bit

I ran away from school today
and now I wish I hadn't
it wasn't that much fun
I got stung by a nettle

I ran away from school today
they told Dad in a letter
he said I shouldn't have
run off without a snack

I ran away from school once too
Dad said, when I was your age
and did you come back?
yes, when it was dinnertime

animal phobia

never in a million years
would I pick up a spider
it's got too many legs
and one might fall off

never in a million years
would I pick up a frog
it's bound to feel all slimy
and I might drop it

never in a million years
would I pick up a bee
it's got too much work to do
and I'd be interrupting

never in a million years
would I pick up a snake
it's good at getting tangled up
and I'm no good at knots

never in a million years
would I pick up a scorpion
it's only got one sting
and that would be a waste

time

why do people say time is ticking by
when it doesn't make a sound?
the clock pretends to know the time
but only when you wind it up
and when it stops, Gran tuts
and says, at least it's right
twice a day

why do people say you tell the time
when it doesn't need to be told?
the sun gets up all by itself
and goes to bed without anyone
telling it to, before Gran's even
made you marmite sandwiches or
read a story

why does Gran say time is a healer
when it's often really mean?
if you're tired or sad or hungry
it goes on and on and winds you up
it slows down when you're bored
and gets faster when you're playing
a fun game

treehouse

today I'm making a treehouse
but first I need a tree
it's got to be a good one
that's twice as big as me

it needs a lot of branches
but not too many leaves
otherwise you can't see out
like you can in Grandpa Steve's

I've got four planks of wood
to make a nice strong floor
and an old kitchen cupboard
to make into a door.

I'm going to get the ladder now
and some of Andy's nails
he says he's got a hammer too
in case my toy one fails.

the planks are kind of heavy
so Andy climbs up first
he hammers til he bangs his thumb
but that's not the worst

the tree I picked was rotten
its branches snapped in two
Andy fell off the ladder
and broke his hammer too

so now I'm making a table
with the kitchen cupboard door
and Grandpa Steve is coming round
to tell the tree what for!

jumpy heart

my heart is jumpy today
going crazy inside my chest
it does that sometimes
but they never know why

the nurses get these stickers out
to stick all over me and then
they clip on coloured wires
but I never know why

doctors ask me questions and
listen to my heart with a cold circle
the machine spits out jagged mountains
but they don't know why

the room is full of beeping
and lots of things on wheels
the lines go weirdly up and down
but I don't know why

they give me pills and puffers
and plastic cups of water
it's like something's going to happen
but they don't know why

so me and my jumpy heart
decide to have a talk
I ask it why it's being crazy
but it doesn't know why

I tell it lots of stories
and my heart starts listening
it's still a little stroppy though
and I don't know why

the machine beside my bed
stops beeping and the mountains
are more like hills now
they still don't know why

the nurses take away the wires
and say I can go home, now
my heart is feeling quieter
if only we knew why

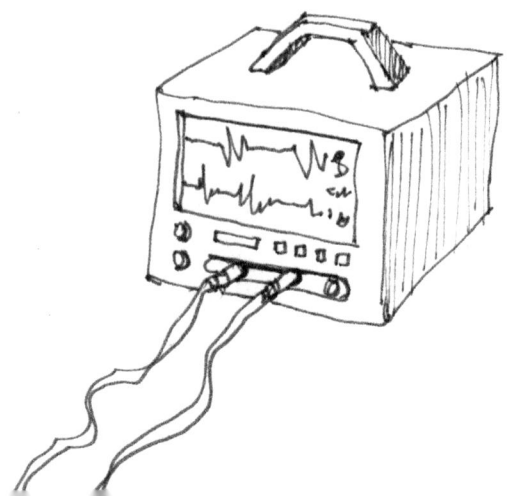

advice for campers

when you go camping
don't forget the ketchup
otherwise you can taste the burnt sausages

when you go camping
remember to take a big rock
otherwise you can't bash the tent pegs in

when you go camping
don't put your tent up downhill
otherwise all your blood goes down to your toes

when you go camping
don't forget to sleep under your pillow
otherwise the sun will wake you up too early

when you go camping
don't forget that if it rains
never ever touch the sides or you get wet

when you go camping
remember to take your toothbrush
otherwise Dad will make you chew a twig instead

when you go camping
take a waterproof jumper and a waterproof book
and make sure your wellies still fit

outage outrage

something isn't right at our house
the internet's stopped working
the tv's on the blink
our phones wont charge
and Dad can't think
what's the matter

we turn off all the plugs
and switch them on again
it makes a weird clink
and sparks rain down
and Dad can't think
what's the matter

he says our house is live
but really should be grounded
he fiddles under the sink
and swears under his breath
cos Dad can't think
what's the matter

he asks our neighbour Jill
if she's got problems too
Jill gives me a friendly wink
I'll get the candles out, she says
cos Dad can't think
what's the matter

another time

sometimes
just before I wake up
I'm in another time before I was born
I'm going on a picnic
I'm driving very fast
there's a baby on the backseat
and it's mine

sometimes
in my other life I'm not even
speaking the same language
my name is Claude or Johann
my house is up a mountain
I know things about medicine
and I am blind

sometimes
my friends are there too
I can hear their voices
but their faces look different
then they turn into wolves
that slope off down the mountain
and I am alone

medal

my mum has a medal in her top drawer
it used to belong to her Dad
but really it's my great granddad's medal
I ask her, what did he get it for?
for being brave.

once a year she pins the medal on her coat
outside there's no traffic in the street
and everyone walks down the middle of the road
to the war memorial and we remember
about being brave.

one day, she says, you will wear it
will I march down the street with you Mum?
you'll march with everyone else that's lost someone
they love, and then you'll know
about being brave.

(to be read with clenched teeth)

sometimes I get really mad
it bubbles up inside me
like a big burbling burp
like an angry animal thrashing about
like a fierce fire right in your face

the fire takes over
the animal roars
and the bubble bursts

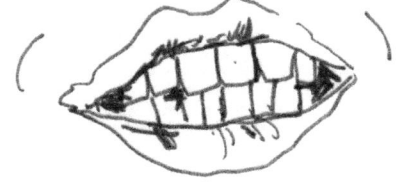

I can't help it
sometimes I just get really mad

Ray's ghost

my friend Ray has a ghost in his house
it lives under the stairs
and when it's in a bad mood
it makes weird noises
thumping and bumping mainly
sometimes scratching and screeching

my friend Ray invited me to tea
but I'm too scared to go
what if the ghost doesn't like me
and makes weird noises
crashing and creaking around?
it'll give me horrible, terrible dreams

my friend Ray didn't come to school today
I bet it's because the ghost
scared him so much it made him
hide in his wardrobe
he's been whimpering and wailing all day
but the ghost couldn't care less

dustbinman

he comes every Friday
in his orange suit with silver stripes
and he looks like a space man

he wheels our bin out
to his truck with the flashing lights
which tips it up like a fairground ride

then he jumps inside the cab
gives me a friendly wave
and drives off down the next street

one day when I'm older
I'll take away everyone's rubbish
on Fridays in my truck

I'll wear an orange spacesuit
and work the fairground ride
and wave to every kid in town

things that are brilliant

it's brilliant when you wake up
and wiggle your toes
when you kick off your duvet
and feel a tickle in your nose
that turns into an e-nor-mous
S N E E Z E !

it's brilliant when your dog
licks your hands and feet
when you're late for school
and you give him a dog treat
that makes him do a hu-mung-ous
W O O F !

it's brilliant when your friends
laugh out loud at your jokes and
when you get to the punch line
your best friend pokes you
in the ribs and you do a gi-gan-tic
H I C C U P !

tall story

in a caravan
in a field
on a farm
on an island
in the middle
of nowhere
was where we
went on holiday
in the caravan
in the field
on the farm
on the island
in the middle
of nowhere
was a very
funny smell
because
under the caravan
in the field
on the farm
on the island
in the middle
of nowhere
was a very
dead sheep

dogs in cars

dogs love cars
they really do
they love jumping into the boot
they love steaming up the windows
they love finding stale crisps
they love making muddy paw prints
on the seats and most of all
they love sticking their head out of the window
and letting the air lick their tongue
as it whooshes past

sister selfie

my sister Carly has spots
but no one knows
because she hides them
under her make up
it takes her a long time to put on
and lots of sponges and brushes
sometimes a few bad words too
but every morning when she's done
her face shines and shimmers
her eyelashes crimped and curled
her cheeks blushing and blooming
and her lips pout
as she takes a selfie

home alone

if I was in that movie
I'd have way more fun
the house would be made of sweets
just like in Hansel and Gretel
so it wouldn't matter
if the fridge was empty
I'd invite Red Riding Hood over
then put on my scariest hallowe'en costume
so it wouldn't matter
if the Wolf rang the doorbell
we'd play The Hobbit on the X-box
and I'd wear my wizard's hat
so it wouldn't matter
if the Dragon blew fire down the chimney
we'd pile up the cushions under the kitchen table
and make a monster nest to sleep in
so it wouldn't matter
if Sully tried to scare us in the night
and when we woke up
Red Riding Hood would call her Grandma
on WhatsApp to check she was OK

new girl

there's a new girl in my class
she has brown hair, red glasses and blue eyes
and she only talks in Turkish

today I sat next to her at lunchtime
she eats black olives, green beans and white cheese
but she only talks in Turkish

her name is written with two dots and a line
she wrote it with my pink and orange felt-tip pens
and read it out in Turkish

I taught her some new words today
and told her I liked red glasses and black olives
güle güle she said to me in Turkish

tomorrow I will ask her if she wants
to be my best friend and share my felt-tip pens
even if she only talks in Turkish

a lazy story (with no letter e)

what I want in this world is
to do nothing
to say nothing
to try nothing
to just sit and wait for tomorrow

if you said I was making it up
I'd say you don't know what I'm thinking

if you said it's hard to do nothing
I'd say, why not just try

and you might find out too
what you want most in this world

when I'm older

when I'm older
I'll live in a log cabin
and never go shopping
because everything I need
is right there in the woods

when I'm older
I'll live in a windmill
and never buy bread
because I'll grind my own flour
and bake loaves in the oven

when I'm older
I'll live in a lighthouse
and never go to work
because all I need to do
is make sure the light works

when I'm older
I'll live on a fishing boat
and never come ashore
because fish prefer
swimming in the sea

when I'm older
I'll live in a teepee
and never feel alone
because I'll light a campfire
and sing songs all night long

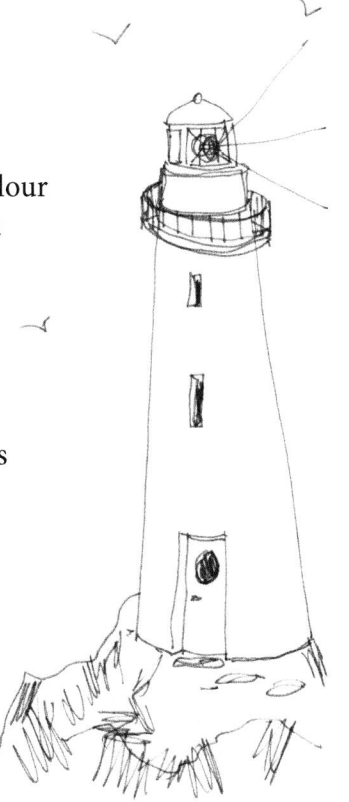

hummus

I like it in sandwiches
I like it on toast
I like it with carrot sticks
I like it most of all
when you scoop it
with your finger
straight from the fridge
but never on a pancake
and never ever hot

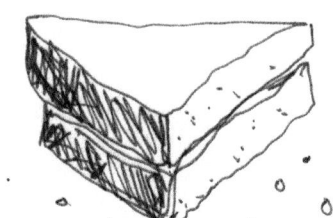

what's in paradise?

sticky buns and chocolate toothpaste
oodles of cuddles and noodles and bubbles
sunshine and snowmen that never go away

and down a little leafy lane
families of goblins and fairies and gnomes
chattering and making funny faces at you

how do you know?
because I've been there

weird, actually

she's weird
he's weird
they're all weird, actually

she wears socks in bed
(her feet might get cold)
he eats biscuits upsidedown
(it tastes the same)

I'm weird
you're weird
we're all weird, actually

apostrophe, catastrophe

you're right
they're sorry
are you sure
that's all?

your right
their sorry
I'm not sure
at all!

let's see if you're right
it's your right to know
let's see if they're sorry
because their 'sorry'
is just an apology
that's all

last Christmas

last Christmas
Bella gave birth
it was just like Jesus
but instead of a baby
there were six puppies
on Christmas morning

bundles of joy
Nanna called them
pain in the neck
moaned my Dad
while Mum and I
just stared in wonder

can we keep them
shall we name them
will Bella feed them
do we need them
that's enough now
let's leave them be

last Christmas
opening presents
eating turkey and stuffing
and too many chocolates
was nothing compared
to Bella's puppies

seabean

cloudforest flower
big as a chandelier
opens its petals
and bats fly in

long bean pod
big as a sword
snaps open
and beans fall out

shiny seabean
small as a pebble
floats across the sea
and lands on a beach

clever seabean
has not forgotten
cracks open
and sends out roots

magpie

beady eye
spies prize

flies down
struts around

pecking picking
black white

scared off
birds scatter

squirrel stays
stares back

magpie mutters
red alert

black white
flaps away

shiny penny
lies forgotten

on Sundays

the teacher has thirty pupils
she asks them to write down
what happens on Sundays

the butcher has fresh meat
he wraps it up in paper
but his shop is closed on Sundays

the farmer has a gun
he keeps it locked away
and shoots clay pigeons on Sundays

the vicar has a sermon
he writes all week
and tells us it on Sundays

the mother has four children
but she can only feed three
so she goes without on Sundays

playing

when you're playing
you're far away
in a desert
under the sea
on Mars

little things become
bigger things
that come and go
in the game
or not at all

the bed is a cloud
a box is a car
it's all up to
your imagination
to decide

if it's going dark
you're in a wood
and your torch
is a cyclops
spying on you

playing is scary
as well as fun
it all makes sense
until someone else
wants to play too

jeepers creepers!

jeepers creepers!
hell's bells!
balls Grandpa
tucked up in bed,
where's my cup of tea?

gordon bennett!
good for nothing!
moans Grandma
coming up stairs,
I've only one pair of legs!

heaven forbid!
well whadda yer know!
yells Grandpa
from the greenhouse,
have you seen what's sprouted?

goodness gracious!
what a sight for sore eyes!
murmurs Grandma
looking through the window,
never thought I'd see the day!

when my hair grows long

when my hair grows long
I'll have a thousand plaits
with beads and bows
and glittery slides

when my hair grows long
I'll have a big bristly brush
to get all the tangles out
and keep it silky

I'll grow it so long
I can sit on it
it'll be longer than
a mermaid's hair

and if we run out of money
I'll cut it off and sell it
and give the money
to my Mum.

London

over London
planes circle
wingtips winking
wheels waking
waiting to land

round London
cars circle
lanes sluggish
lorries slowish
waiting to move

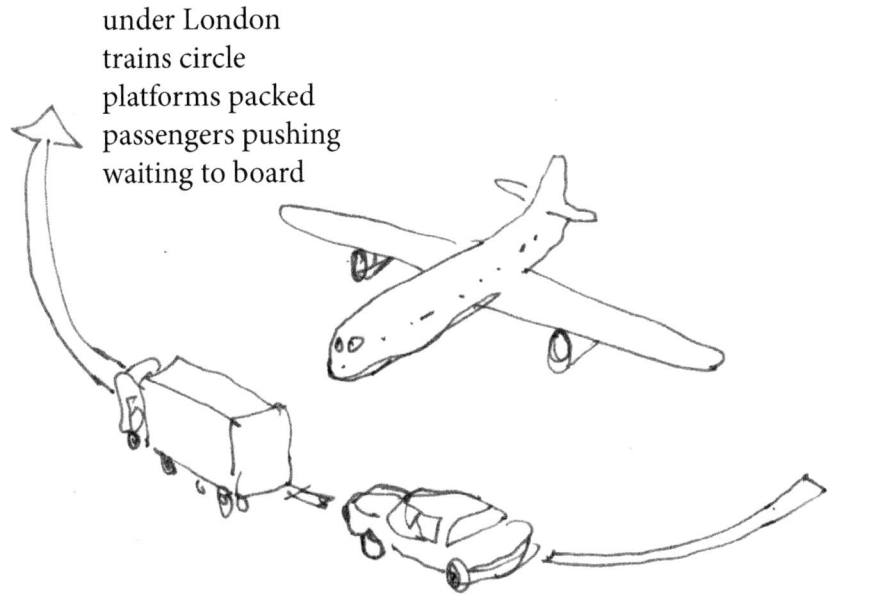

under London
trains circle
platforms packed
passengers pushing
waiting to board

wrong names

if Iceland is green
and Greenland is icy
shouldn't they just switch?

call Iceland Greenland
and Greenland Iceland
and make new maps

it might take a while
for the new names to sink in
that's what I'm worried about

and what if Iceland gets icy
and Greenland melts
because of climate change?

they'd have to switch
the names back to what
they were before

indoor voices

our teacher doesn't mind
when we shout outdoors
she calls it letting off steam
and on very cold days
you can even see it!

but when we come inside
and hang up our coats
she says we have to use
our indoor voices
otherwise the walls will shake
and the windows will rattle
and things might break

like when a lady sings
in a very loud voice
and suddenly a glass shatters
into a million pieces because
she's letting off too much steam

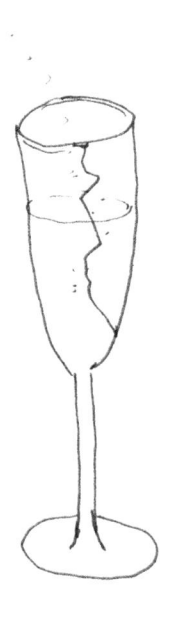

in the loft

what's up there Dad?
all sorts of rubbish
why is it dark up there?
because the light bulb broke
why does the ladder make funny noises?
because it hates me going up there
what are you looking for?
something your mother wants down
do you know where it is?
no.

is it up there Dad?
your mother says it is
how are you going to find it?
well it's up there somewhere
is it with the Christmas decorations?
I jolly well hope not
is it in a box with a label on it?
not in a million years
can I climb the ladder and help you look?
no.

babies

babies are cute
and sort of coo
babies are small
and smell of poo

babies are noisy
and cry all night
babies are funny
and like to fight

babies are boring
and sleep a lot
babies are happy
and full of snot

babies are strong
and grow quite quick
babies are ticklish
and are often sick

babies are lovely
when they are clean
but babies take over
if you know what I mean

things I wouldn't do if I were you

never grind black pepper
into an eggcup and then blow into it
it hurts

never make a go-cart
and then stand on a rusty nail
it hurts

never touch a chilli pepper
and then touch your eye
it hurts

never stroke a cactus
that's covered in fuzzy spikes
it hurts

never go the wrong way
through a revolving door
it hurts

never leave your violin
in the garden overnight
it hurts

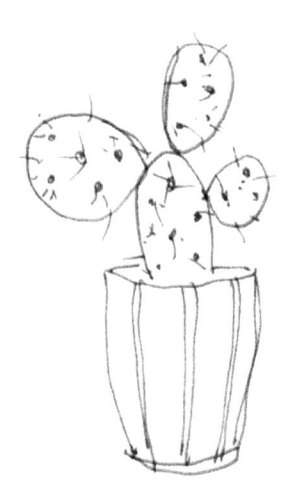

monopoly

my brother loves it
but my sister hates it
what's the point? she says
I want to win! he says

my sister groans
but my brother wants to play
it's only toy money! she says
I know! he says

my brother picks the car
and my sister takes the iron
the houses are plastic! she says
I don't care! he says

my sister rolls the dice
and my brother lands in jail
it's not a real prison! he says
I know! she says

my brother is losing
and my sister has Mayfair
can I owe you? he says
no, I win! she says

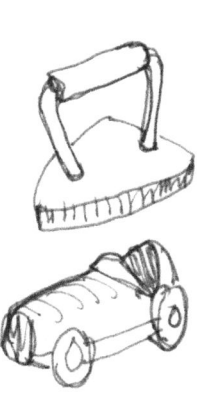

a poem about running

some people go running
when they need time to think
they say it clears their head
of all the cobwebs

some people go running
when they've eaten too much
they say in January it gets rid
of all the Christmas pudding

some people go running
when they want to get fit
they feel energy coming out
of all their new muscles

but when I go running
I'm on a pavement adventure
I can feel stories coming out
of all the homes and hedges

fireworks

I'd really like to know
how they get all those
exploding colours and patterns
into a tube the size of a toilet roll
I'd really like to know
how they lay them out
in a big muddy field
and light them so they
all go off in order
and set the sky on fire
I'd really like to know
what makes the bangs and whistles
inside a tube the size of a toilet roll
and where it all goes
when it's over

snow

to us it's just white
arriving cold and unexpected
it makes us dance and giggle
it makes good snowballs
it changes the sounds
and changes the light
that's all snow is

to eskimos it's something more
and has lots of different names
depending on what it's used for
some snow is good for making igloos
packed down hard and cut into blocks
with your long sharp hunting knife
some snow is good for riding on
packed up warm and riding on a sleigh
with your eager pack of huskies
some snow is good for getting news
packed into its icy cracks
are signs of spring

mazes

mazes are amazing
don't you think?
you can spend hours
running into deadends
trying to find the middle

left right
wrong
right left
I'm here!

and when you get there
it's fun listening to
everyone getting lost
peeping through hedges
trying to find the middle

left right
wrong
right left
I'm here!

some mazes are made of maize
some are made of bronze
and some are in puzzle books
you use your pencil
to try to find the middle

duffel coat

when my Dad started school
his Mum bought him a duffel coat
it was thick and stiff
and had awkward toggly buttons
shaped like rugby balls

when my Dad got to school
he didn't like his duffel coat
it was hot and heavy
and the awkward toggly buttons
wouldn't come undone

when his teacher helped him out
Dad started to like his duffel coat
it looked cosy and clean
with its awkward toggly buttons
just hanging on his peg

when it was time to go home
Dad put on his navy duffel coat
it was his and it was home time
and the awkward toggly buttons
didn't matter any more

TV animals

TV animals roam the land
carefree and strong
they have plenty to eat
and somewhere to live
and they don't die

TV animals groom each other
perfect and happy
they belong to prides and herds
they feed and wash and preen
and they don't die

but what happens to TV animals
when they turn the cameras off
when a monkey gets stuck
when a gazelle goes hungry
when an antelope gets attacked
and they die?

beans on toast

if you're just back from holiday
if you're kept off school
if you get home late
if you've run out of fuel
- beans on toast!

if your fridge is empty
if you've just moved in
if your best friend hates you
if you're soaked to the skin
- beans on toast!

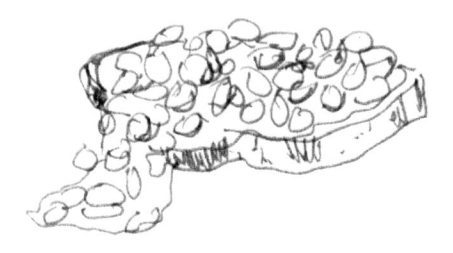

spider's web

watch her dangle on a thread
swinging across the glade
watch her walk a tightrope
that she's just made

watch her make the spokes
spinning through the air
watch her walk between them
how does she dare?

flimsy and intricate
she weaves in and out
then nestles in the middle
to see who's about

a fly barges into it
in spite of its big eyes
she wraps him up for breakfast
with invisible lies

here are a few pages for you to write your own poems

SARAH HOLDING
lives in a funny old house with
a leaning tower on the outskirts
of London with her husband
and their three children.
She is the author of the children's
time travel adventure trilogy
SeaBEAN and a young adult cli-fi
novel set during the fall of Atlantis,
entitled **CHAMELEON**.
She loves long train journeys,
drinking coffee, cooking vegan
food and playing the saxophone.
This is her first collection of poetry.

sarah-holding.com

Sarah Holding offers inspirational talks
and poetry workshops for schools,
both online and in person.
For more information email:
bookings@sarah-holding.com